Regulate with

Kids' Regulation Tips, from A-Z

Illustrated by Jason Viviers

Copyright © 2024 Nisi Cohen

All rights reserved.

No portion of this book may be used or reproduced in any form without written permission from the author.

This publication is designed to provide accurate and authoritative information concerning the subject matter covered. It is sold with the understanding that the author is not engaged in rendering professional services. The advice and strategies contained herein may not be suitable for your child's situation and are not intended to replace professional medical advice. The reader must consult with the relevant health professionals for individualized guidance regarding their child.

Published & Printed by Amazon Kindle Direct Publishing

Book Layout and Cover Design by Jason Viviers
Illustrations by Jason Viviers

First edition April 2024

This book is dedicated to:
Asher – Our source of endless joy and laughter
Kate – The world's best nervous system healer
And Gadi – Thank you for all the encouragement, love, and of course, coffee.

Dear Grown-up,

I'm thrilled you've chosen to explore this book with the young ones in your care!

In the pages that follow, you'll be introduced to Kate, Sofia, Max, and Cole. Together, you'll embark on a journey of regulation. Along the way you'll learn fun and effective strategies for self-regulating (achieving a 'just right' state). This book is ideally for kids between the ages of 5 and 10 years old, and it may serve as a valuable resource for neurodivergent children, experiencing self-regulation challenges.

Equipping our children with regulation tools is one of the best ways to help them develop flexibility, confidence and resilience. It is my hope that our young readers will experiment with the techniques shared in this book and will discover how to become the best version of themselves.

Happy reading. Here's to a journey of discovery and growth!

Nisi

Disclaimer: Although I'm proudly South African, I've tailored this book's spelling to accommodate U.S. readers.

In a world that's confusing, wacky, and wild,
It's really not easy being a child.
We get all muddled and can't think straight,
When we're antsy, anxious, or just in a state!

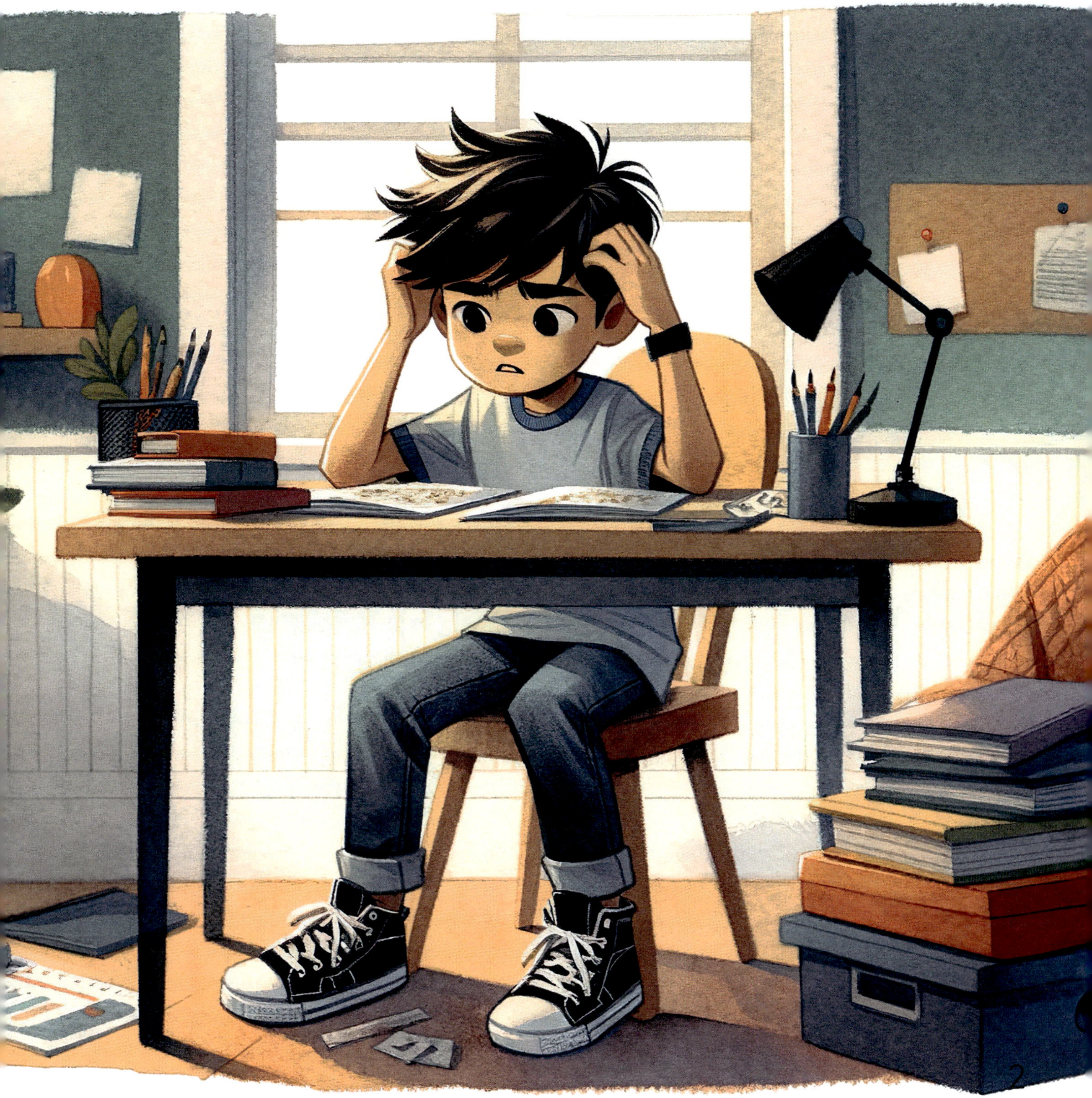

Have you heard of this "REGULATION" idea?
It's a way to reset and get back into gear!

Now let's get acquainted—my name is Kate.
Join my crew as we learn how to regulate.
Together with Max, Sofia, and Cole,
We'll discover great ways to get back in control.

Cole Kate Sofia Max

So, find a good spot and explore these pages
With A-to-Z tips for kids of all ages!

6

Becoming **AWARE**—here I'll start my quest
To recognize when I'm not feeling my best.

Once I **ACCEPT** that something's amiss,
I can find different ways of handling this!

I take a deep **BREATH** and carefully track
How my body feels—from front to **BACK**.
From my head to my toes, I get a sense
Which limbs are feeling twitchy or tense.

8

I can lie on my **BED** or sit on the floor,
Scanning my **BODY** to find out more...
Is my heart pounding or skipping a beat?
Do I have a sore tummy or fidgety feet?

I carry on breathing and **CLOSE** my eyes,
Allowing my belly to fall and rise.

I **COUNT** one to ten—nice and slow,
Feeling more **CALM** as I start to let go.

Footnote for Adults: Body-Scanning is a type of mindfulness meditation where the person notices how each part of their body feels, without any judgement.

10

I can **DRAW** on some paper or **DOODLE** instead,
To **EMPTY** the worries and thoughts from my head.

I check my **EMOTIONS**—how I feel inside,
And name **EACH** feeling, with an adult to guide.

12

Whatever I **FEEL** is totally **FINE**!
It's okay to have wobbles from time to time.

It just makes me human—I know it's not bad
To be angry, annoyed, worried, or sad!

14

15

I look out for **GLIMMERS** to perk up my mood,
Like laughing or eating my favorite food.
Listening to music, cuddling my pet,
Playing fun **GAMES** with friends that I've met.

Picnics outside, a warm gentle breeze,
Catching a **GLIMPSE** of the sun through the trees.

GRABBING these moments will slowly retrain,
My sensory system, my body, and brain!

Footnote for Adults: Glimmers are little moments of joy or amazement. Tuning into positive feelings and sensations during these moments help to reset and calm the nervous system (Refer to Deb Dana's The Polyvagal Theory in Therapy).

Something I love to do before bed
Is making a **GRATITUDE** list...in my head!

I think of all of the people I love,
The park and the playground, the blue skies above.
My talents and hobbies, my friends, and my teachers,
My books about heroes and magical creatures!

Footnote for Adults: Expressing gratitude doesn't magically erase one's worries or stresses. But if done regularly, this activity rewires the brain towards a more positive outlook and triggers the release of hormones such as oxytocin which improves one's ability to cope in stressful situations, thereby facilitating greater resilience.

18

Nourishing, **HEALTHY** food on my plate,
HEADING to bed before it gets late,
Drinking fresh water and playing outdoors,
Keeping things tidy and **HELPING** with chores.

The adults around me love to explain,
How these **HABITS** are great for my body and brain!

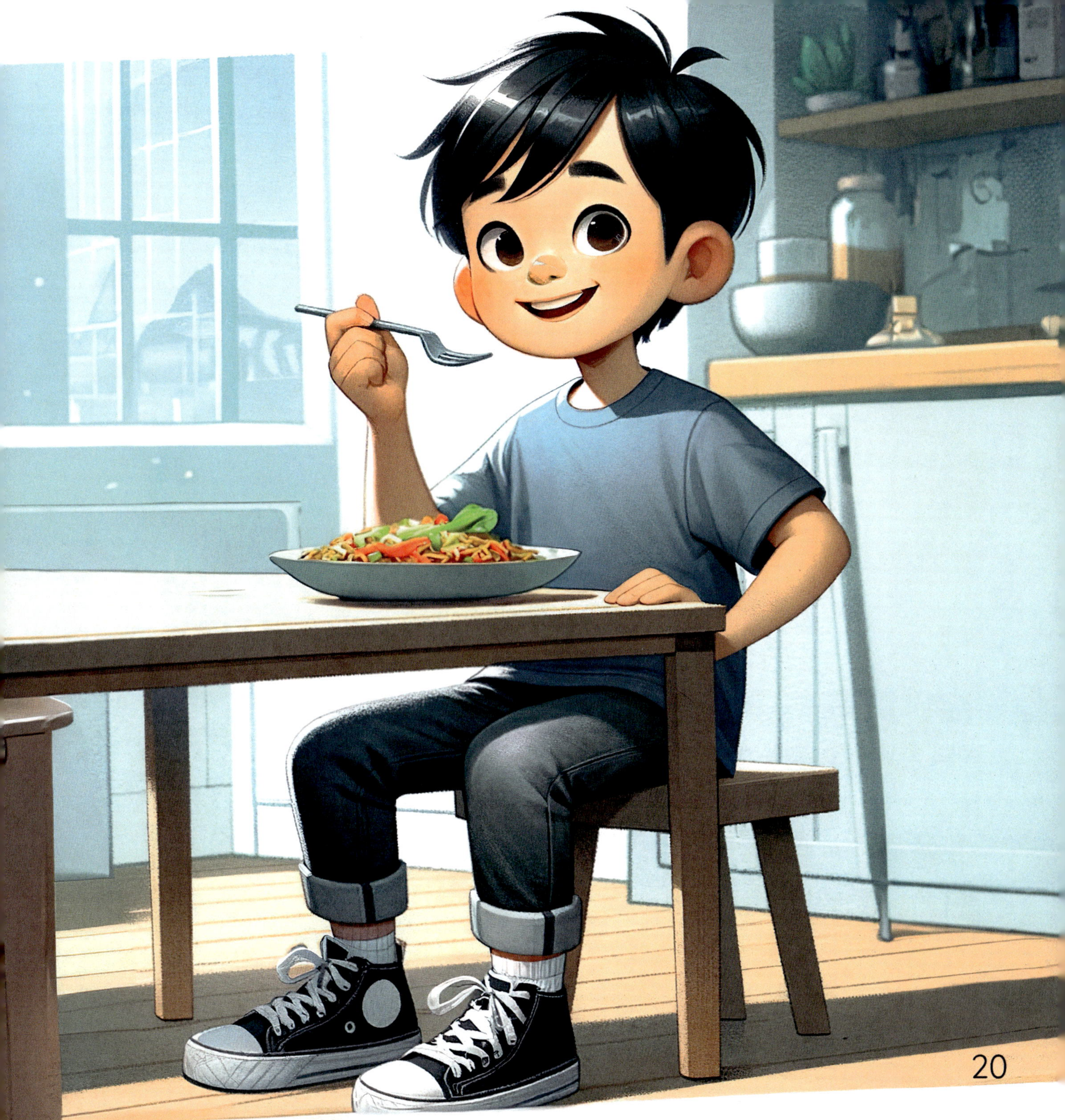

21

When I'm all rattled and my heart starts to race,
I **IMAGINE** myself in a beautiful place.

An enchanted forest with fireflies,
Or a jungle with rivers and misty gray skies,
Maybe an island, by a shimmering sea,
Picture yourself anywhere—try it with me!

JUST a reminder—this **JOURNEY** we're on
Is much more fun when we pass **JOY** along.

It's really important to donate and share,
And to treat every person with **KINDNESS** and care.
Giving out blankets, clothing, or food—
Spreading **LOVE** is a sure way to **LIFT** your mood!

24

When I'm not winning with regulation,
There's a **METHOD** I use—it's called **MEDITATION**.
With help from an adult, I can find it online,
Then follow directions, one step at a time.

I breathe through my nose, very slowly... then sigh—
Thoughts drifting away like clouds in the sky.

Even five **MINUTES** can help me reset.
Have you tried out this little trick yet?

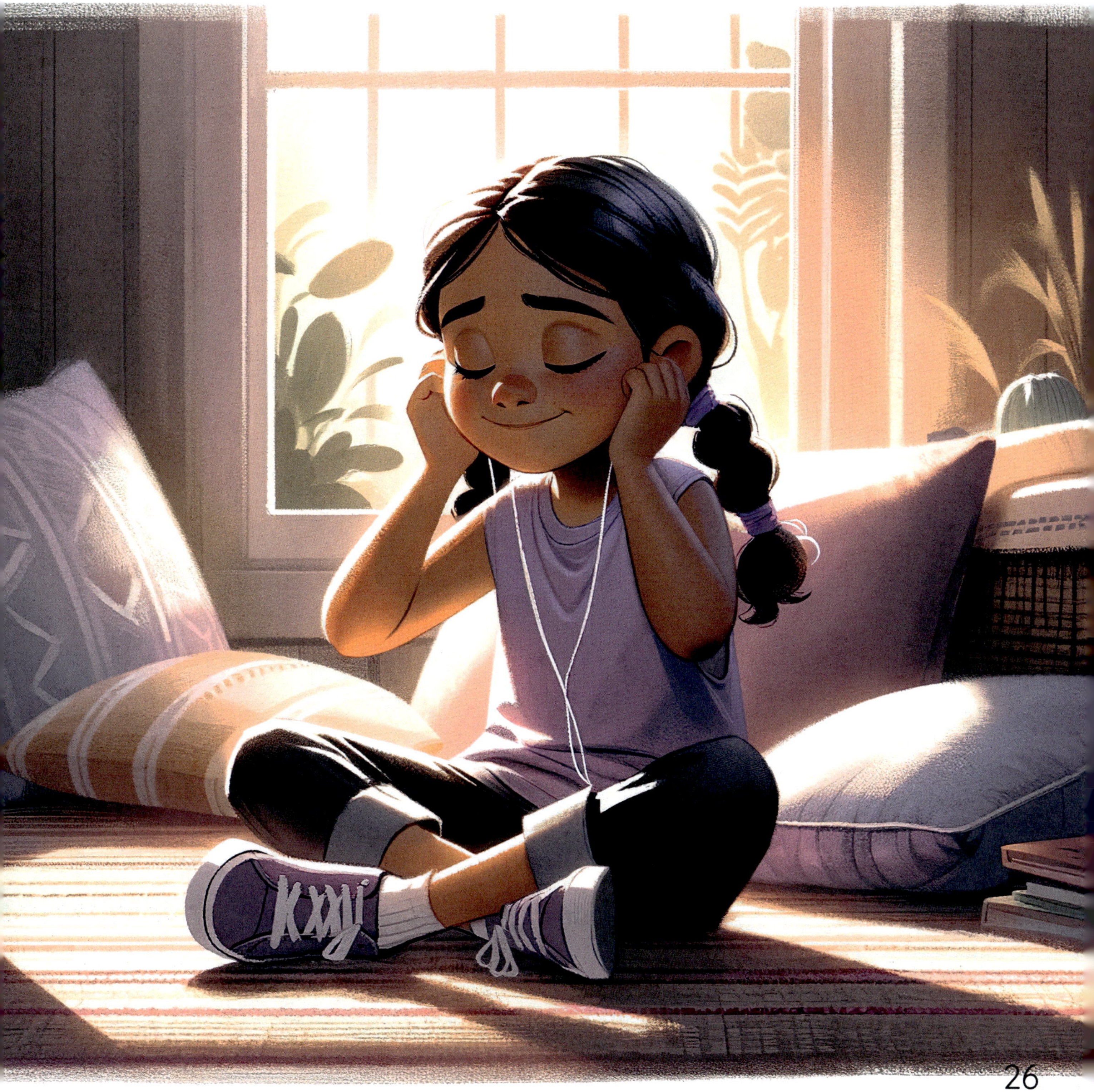

Spending time in **NATURE**, I leave my stress behind,
Walking in the crisp fresh air helps to calm my mind.
With a grown-up there to watch me... keeping a close eye,
I take a stroll to **NEIGHBORS** or visit friends **NEARBY**.

Some kids live **NEAR** forests, or mountains or the beach,
But for lots of children, these spots are out of reach.
That's really **NOT** a problem, since nature's all around,
Just head outside and **NIMBLY** get your feet onto the ground!

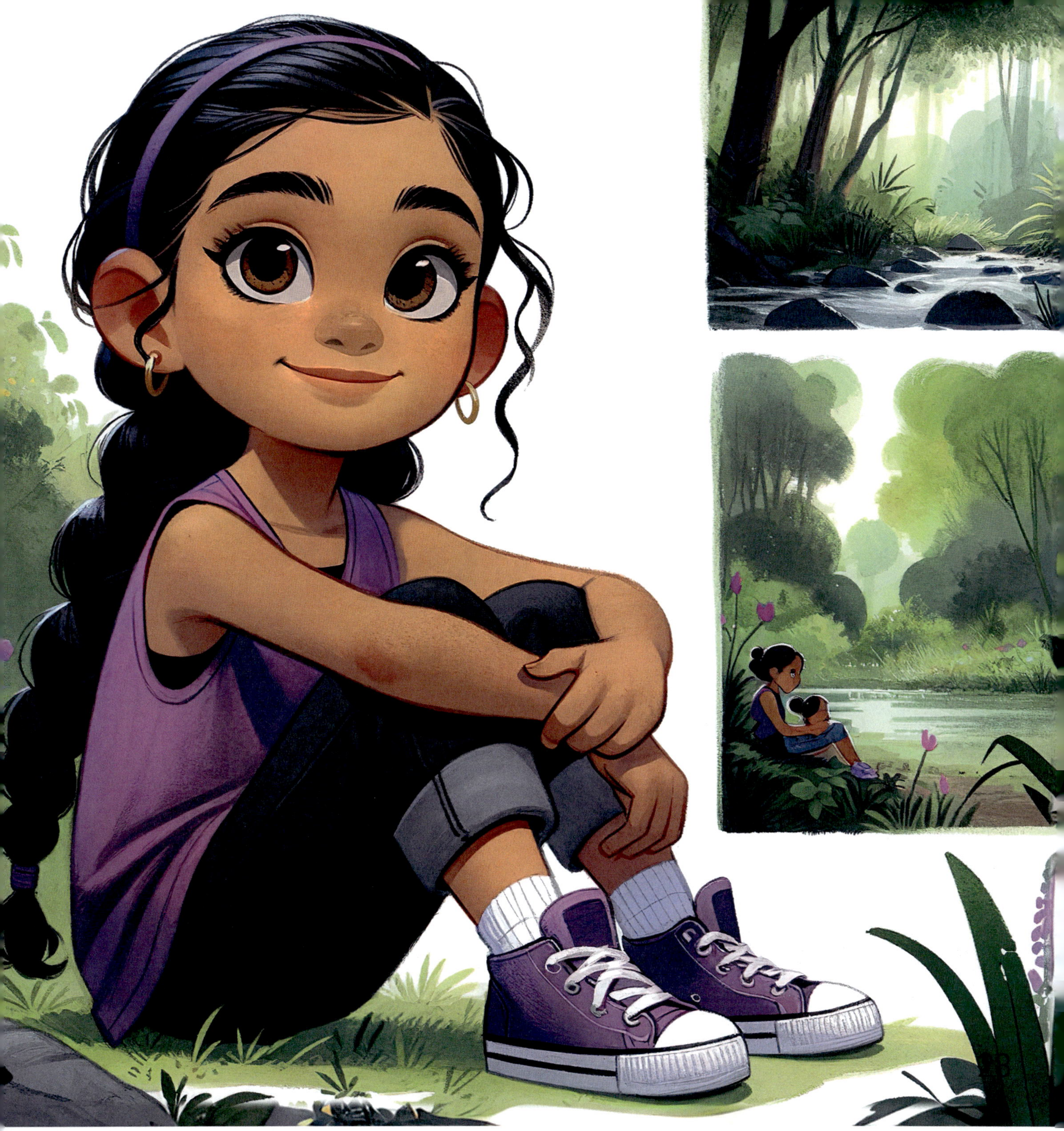

I try to be an **OPTIMIST**—holding **ONTO** hope,
Even when I'm **OUT** of sorts and want to moan or mope.

OH I know it isn't easy on days that bring dismay,
But I tell myself, no matter what, it's going to be **OKAY**!

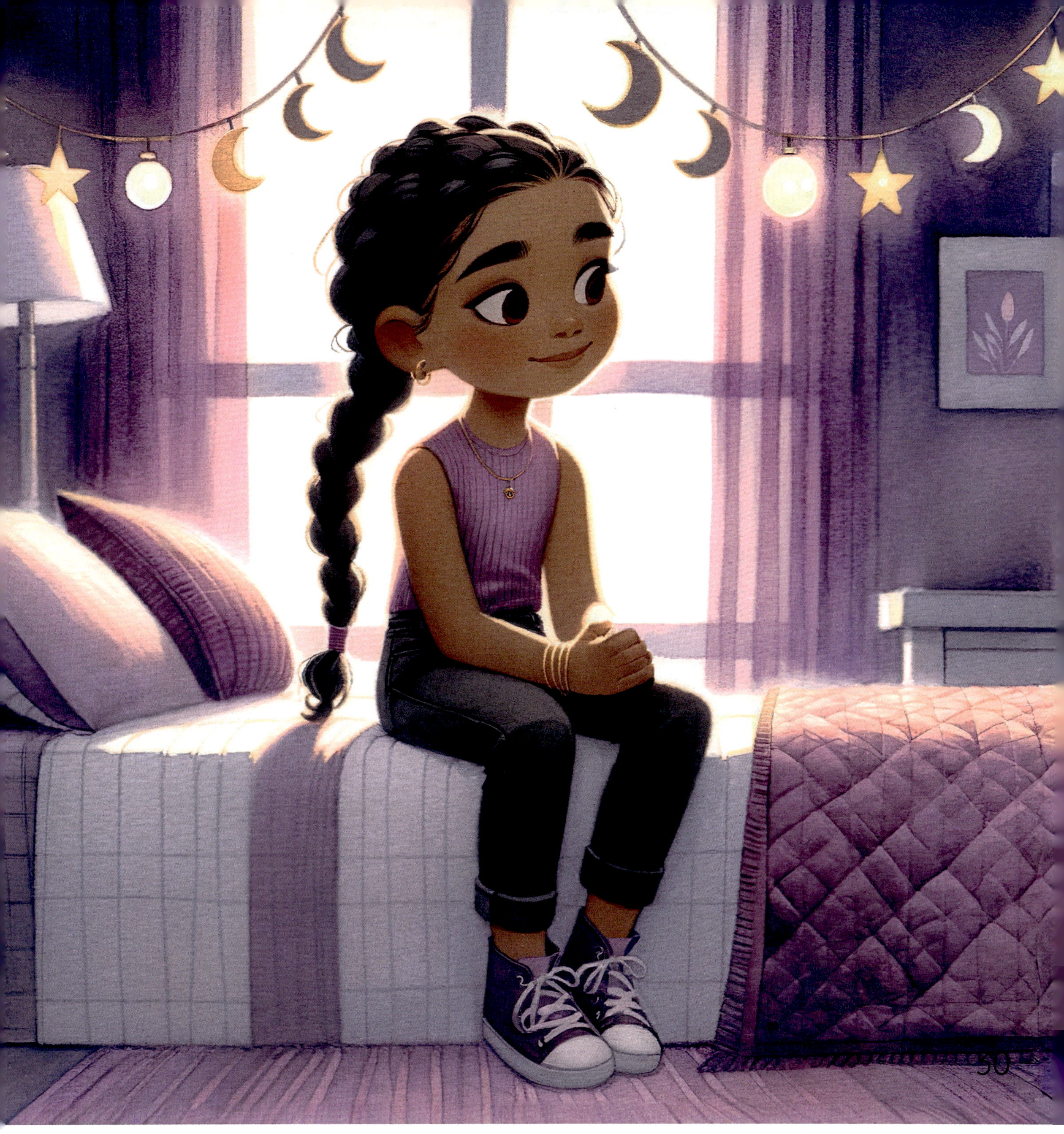

31

Getting out and **PLAYING**—the best part of my routine—
My chance to move and run around—a nice break from the screen!

At the **PARK** and **PLAYGROUND**, I cycle, swing, and slide.
I always feel my very best after time outside!

Adults like to exercise—it keeps them fit and slim.
Well, did you know that kids like me can also hit the gym?

PUSH-UPS, **PLANKS**, and star-jumps—super fun to do,
These exercises make me strong and regulate me too!

Footnote for Adults: This kind of physical activity would take place under the supervision of an occupational therapist (OT) or physical therapist (PT). Specific exercises and equipment would be chosen to cater to each child's needs.

34

Each night, I get good **QUALITY** sleep—it's the only way
To help **RESTORE** my tired brain from a long and busy day!

I try to be well-**RESTED** so that I can **REGULATE**,
And feel **READY** to race off to school, in a happy state!

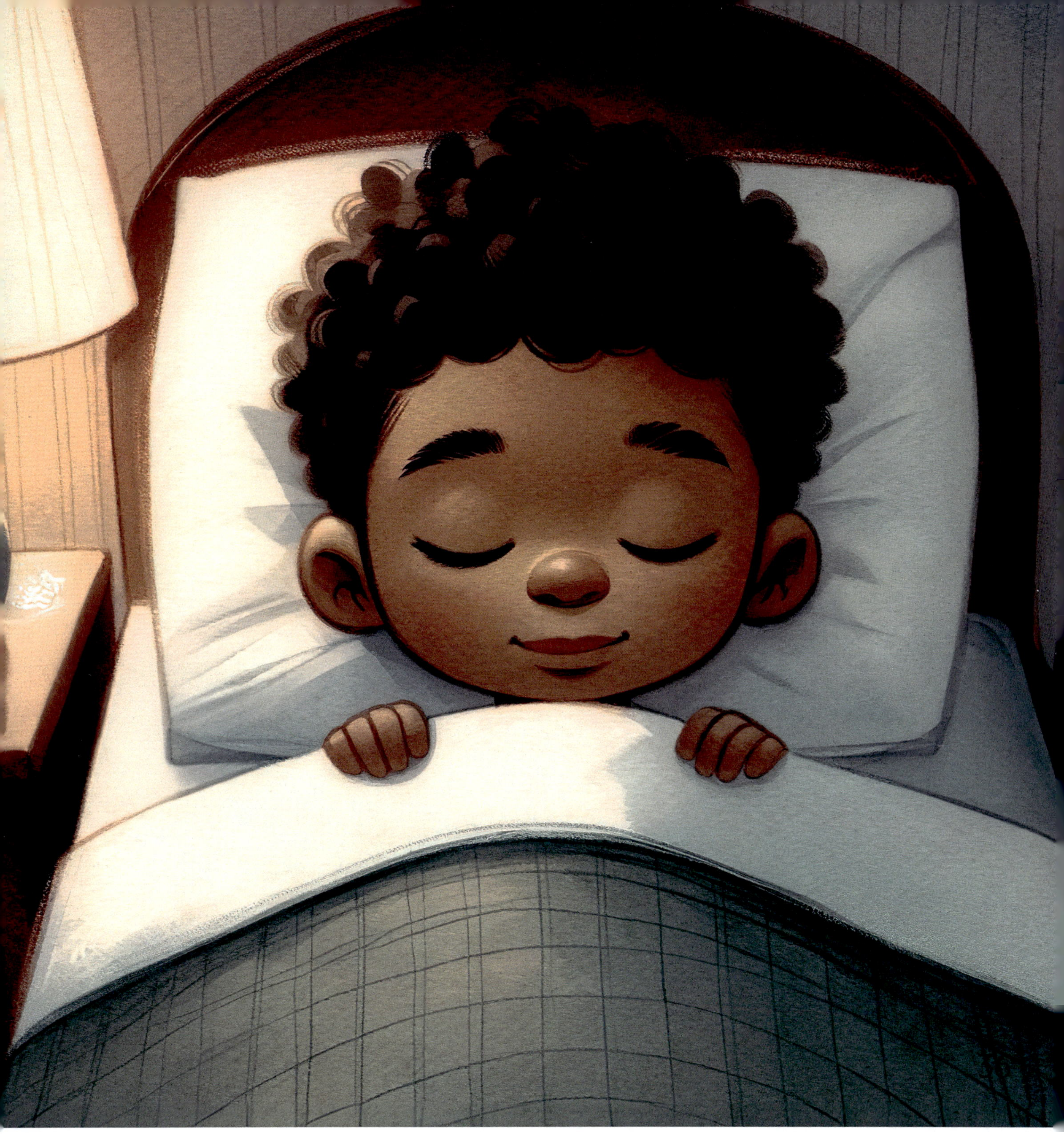

I sometimes need a **SAFE SPACE** where I can be alone,
A cozy place to **SETTLE**, in my classroom or at home.

A **SIMPLE** little reading nook or a calm and private **SPOT**.
SPENDING time inside my tent really helps a lot!

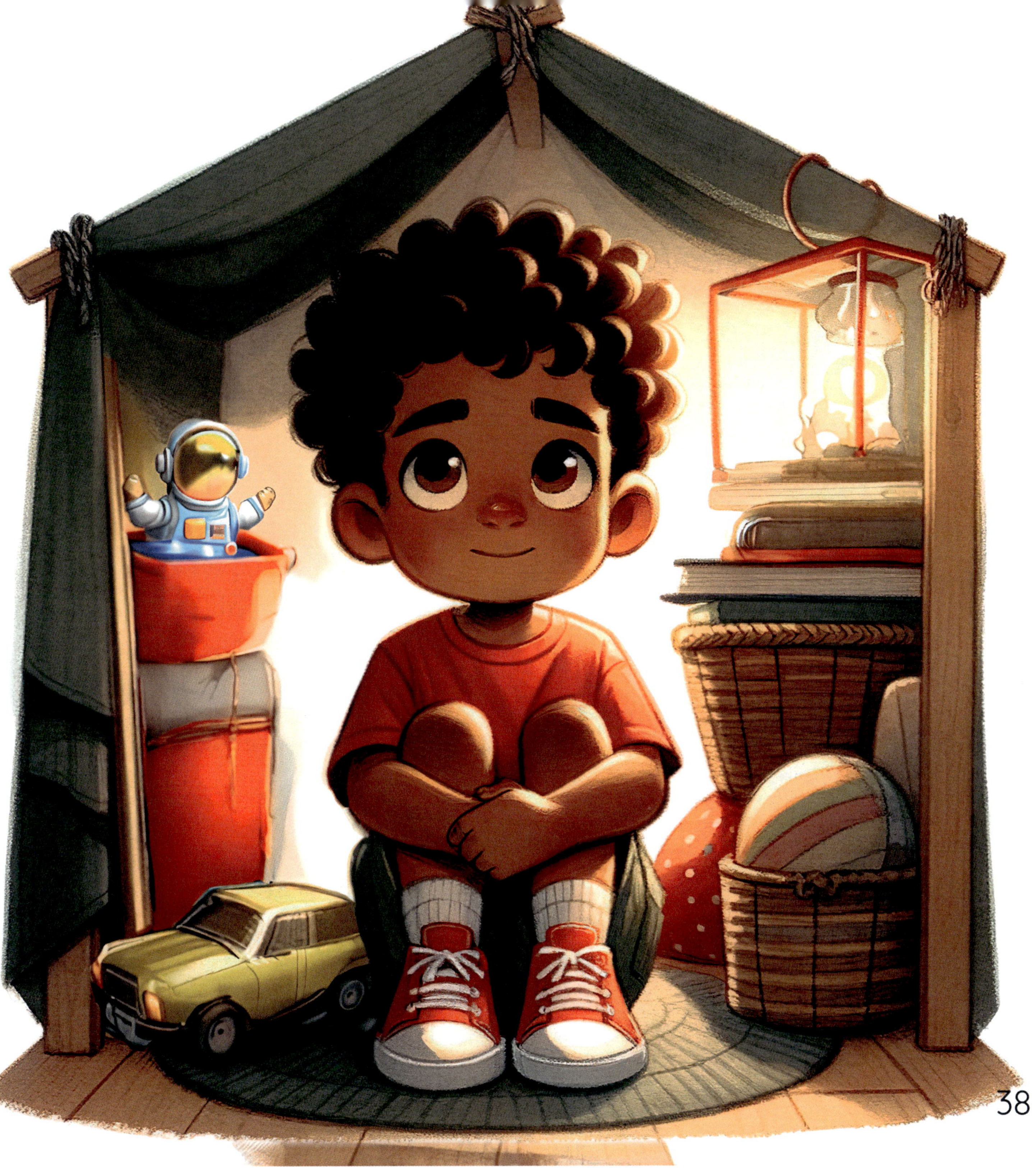

I often ask a **THERAPIST** or **TEACHER** that I **TRUST**
To hear me out and help me—to guide me when I'm fussed.

They **TRULY UNDERSTAND** me and are so **VERY** kind,
When I need to cry or **VENT**, and say what's on my mind.

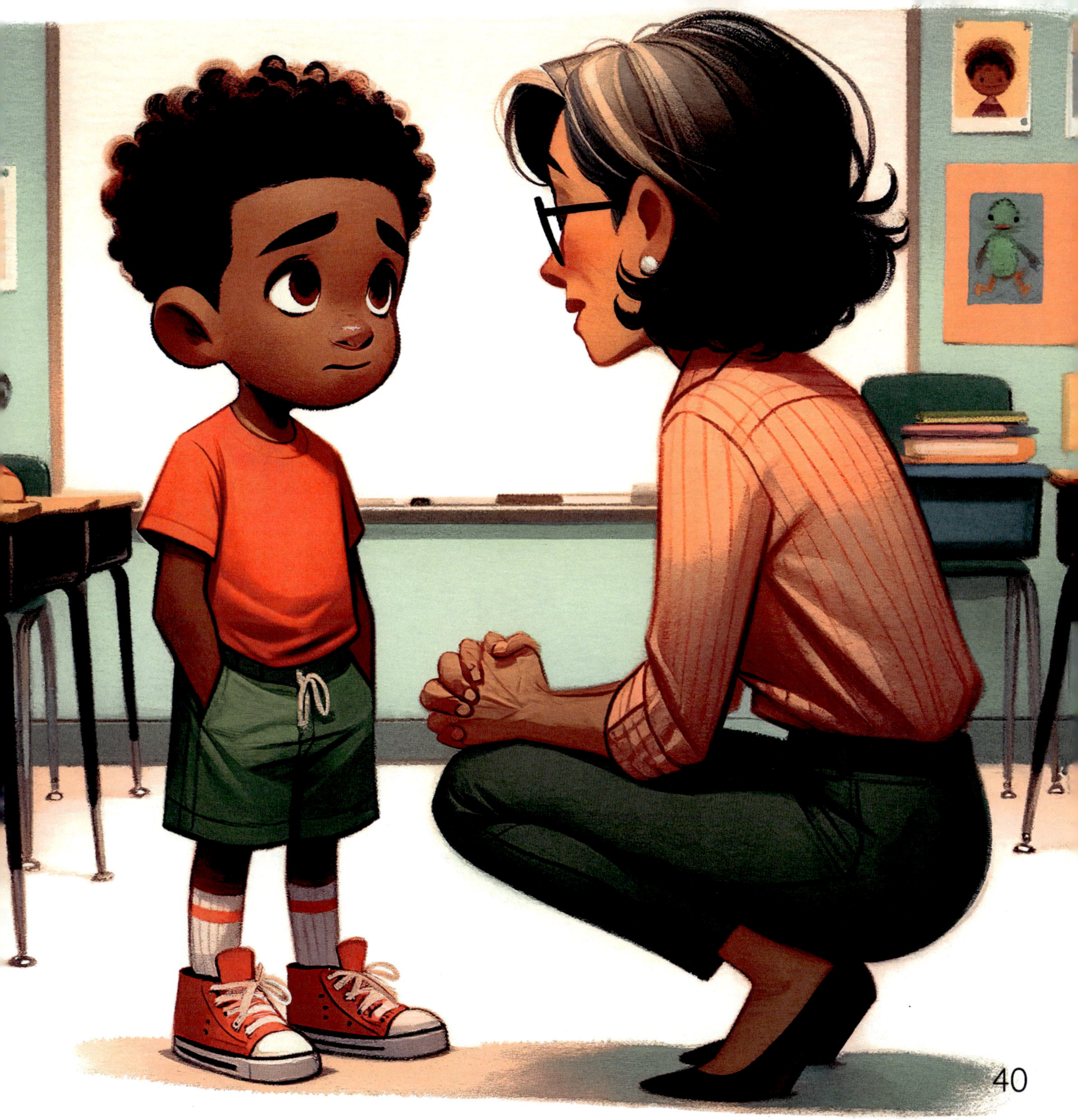

41

I hope you'll **WANT** to try out all the **WAYS** that we've E**XPLORED**.
You'll E**XPERIENCE** a whole new **YOU**, a system that's restored.

Trust **YOURSELF** to do your best and practice what we've shown,
That's my final tip to get you in a regulated **ZONE**!

ACKNOWLEDGMENTS

- Jason, thank you for the many hours of work and your unwavering dedication. I'm in awe of your talent and so appreciative of your patience and commitment throughout this process.
- Joy, this book wouldn't have ever been written if it wasn't for your fabulous course, and all the edits and support. Thank you!
- Erica, for the brilliant edits and recommendations.
- Thank you to my parents and sisters, and to Gadi, Esther, Hazel and David for your incredible support, throughout this whole process.
- Last but not least, thank you to my BV family: All the teachers, therapists and of course, Alison Scott. I'm eternally grateful for the knowledge and insights I gained while working with you all. This book was inspired by the beautiful ethos of the school: child-led education, connection before correction, and a culture of care.

A NOTE FOR TEACHERS AND PARENTS

Self-Regulation Challenges are common in children with ADHD, Autism, anxiety, and sensory processing difficulties, as well as those who have experienced trauma and are stuck in the 'fight-flight-freeze-or-fawn' response.

Signs that your child may be dysregulated:
- Severe, frequent tantrums and outbursts
- Low frustration tolerance
- Often refusing to participate in activities at home or school
- Struggling to focus and complete tasks
- Frequent crying or negative moods
- Excessively high energy levels—inability to settle down
- Extremely low energy levels—no motivation to do anything
- Seeking sensory input (e.g., deliberately crashing into objects, moving excessively, tapping or fidgeting)
- Avoiding sensory input (e.g., negative reactions to noise, an aversion to clothing fabrics or certain food textures)

The Purpose Of This Book
This book describes various strategies for enhancing nervous system modulation and emotional regulation. I was inspired to write it as a resource for children who struggle with managing their energetic and emotional state. The purpose of this book is to guide children with techniques or lifestyle modifications that will help them shift into a 'just-right' zone, in which they have greater capacity to 'rest and digest' as well as 'attend and befriend'.

My hope is that, while parents, caregivers and teachers read this book to the little ones in their care, they also pick up a few tips for themselves. At the end of the day, we ALL need tools to help us self-regulate, develop resilience, and thrive .

Nisi is a registered Speech Language Pathologist with over ten years of experience supporting children with ADHD, Dyslexia, Apraxia, and Autism. She is certified as a Multi-Sensory Therapeutic Environment Practitioner and Kids' Yoga instructor, and she is passionate about helping students overcome learning barriers in a holistic and fun way.

In 2024, Nisi founded Nova Co—an online resource hub for parents. Her mission is to empower parents with knowledge and tools to help their neurodivergent children thrive. She believes in using an integrative approach for enhancing communication, learning, and wellbeing. Passionate about neuroscience and child development, Nisi is currently pursuing an MSc degree in Neurodevelopment at the University of the Witwatersrand, South Africa.

For more information and guidance visit her website www.novacokids.com.
You can also follow her @novacokids instagram page for tips and resources.

Made in the USA
Las Vegas, NV
22 June 2024